ENGLISH? YES, PLEASE

Over 1000 illustrated words
with games and activities

EUROPEAN LANGUAGE INSTITUTE

© 1987 - **ELI** s.r.l. - **European Language Institute**
P.O. Box 6 - Recanati - Italy
Tel. 071/750701 - Fax 071/977851
3rd reprint 1995

Printed in Italy by Tecnostampa s.r.l.

ALL RIGHTS RESERVED. NO PART OF THIS PUBLICATION
MAY BE REPRODUCED, STORED IN A RETRIEVAL SYSTEM,
OR TRANSMITTED IN ANY FORM OR BY ANY MEANS, ELECTRONIC,
MECHANICAL, PHOTOCOPYING, RECORDING, OR OTHERWISE,
WITHOUT THE PRIOR WRITTEN PERMISSION OF THE PUBLISHER.

"**English? Yes, please**" is a complement to the ELI comics and faithfully follows their didactic intention, that is, the teaching of foreign languages in a pleasant and amusing way. Prepared by a team of experts in linguistic didactics, this easy and efficient volume is not to be considered a course of English, but an aid, especially in the teaching of vocabulary. In fact, twenty *full-size pictures* illustrate all the main aspects of daily life: from the *house* to the *town,* from *jobs* to *animals* and so on. Each illustration is followed by a page where, beside a small vocabulary illustrating mainly verbs and adjectives, you can find *relevant exercises* and *games* of various types, which require the use of the words in the previous picture. They may be exercises in which the reader, having to answer some questions of the multiple choice type or complete some sentences, must choose from the newly-learned words and/or put them into the right context.

The modern practice of language teaching gives more and more importance to *visualization,* as didactic experts are convinced that an illustrated word is learned in a more immediate and lasting way than a word that is only explained with other words. This is the didactic criterion that has inspired the present publication, which can also be used by students at home, especially *during the holidays,* to *revise* what they have learned during the school year in a very *useful and pleasant way.* "**English? Yes, please**" is ideal reading since it does not oblige students to follow a graded series of units but allows them to use the book freely and choose the pages according to their interests and their learning needs. On the last pages of "**English? Yes, please**" he can check the solutions of the games and find the various exercises completed.

NATURE

Look at the picture carefully and then say if these sentences are RIGHT or WRONG.

1. There's snow on the hill. _____
2. There are two lakes in the picture. _____
3. There's a waterfall on the left of the picture. _____
4. There are flowers on the beach. _____
5. There's a river on the right of the picture. _____
6. There are no bushes in the bay. _____
7. There's a wood in the village. _____

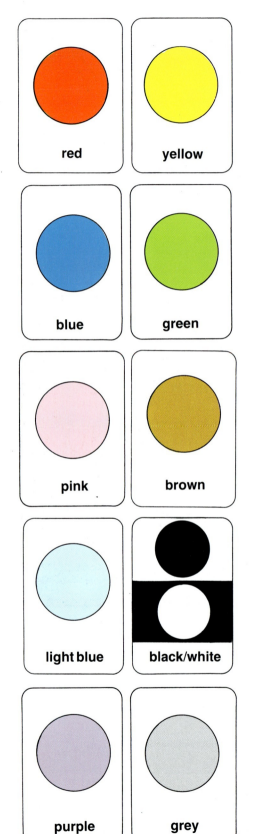

Look for the words listed below in the letter maze. You can go from left to right or right to left, from top to bottom or bottom to top or diagonally in all directions. Score out the words as you find them and then write the remaining letters in the squares below.

- ☐ bay
- ☐ beach
- ☐ bushes
- ☐ cloud
- ☐ hedge
- ☐ hill
- ☐ horizon
- ☐ island
- ☐ lake
- ☐ meadow
- ☐ mountain
- ☐ peak
- ☐ plain
- ☐ pond
- ☐ rocks
- ☐ sea
- ☐ sky
- ☐ snow
- ☐ stream
- ☐ wood

M	E	N	O	Z	I	R	O	H
A	A	K	S	C	L	O	U	D
E	N	E	A	A	Y	K	S	O
R	V	I	S	L	A	N	D	O
T	H	C	A	E	B	N	E	W
S	E	K	A	T	I	T	S	O
D	D	A	L	A	N	N	K	D
N	G	E	L	U	O	U	C	A
O	E	P	I	W	R	E	O	E
P	S	E	H	S	U	B	R	M

**Colour the drawing with the colours corresponding to the numbers:
1. light blue, 2. pink, 3. white, 4. purple, 5. green, 6. brown, 7. blue, 8. grey, 9. yellow, 10. red, 11. black.** Then complete the sentences, using the various colours and words from the picture on pages 6 and 7.
Example: The C L O U D S are P I N K

1. The sky is _ _ _ _ _ _ _ _ _.

2. The _ _ _ _ _ are green.

3. The snow _ _ _ _ _ _ _.

4. The _ _ _ _ _ is blue.

5. The mountains _ _ _ _ _ _ _ _ _.

6. The _ _ _ _ _ _ _ are brown.

7. The rocks are _ _ _ _.

8. The _ _ _ _ _ _ _ are _ _ _.

THE TOWN

Answer the questions (yes or no)

1. Is the tower near the Town Hall? ....
2. Is the school near the railway station? ....
3. Is the skyscraper near the church? ....
4. Is the newspaper kiosk near the filling station? ....
5. Is the store near the shop? ....
6. Is there a sign-board on the house? ....

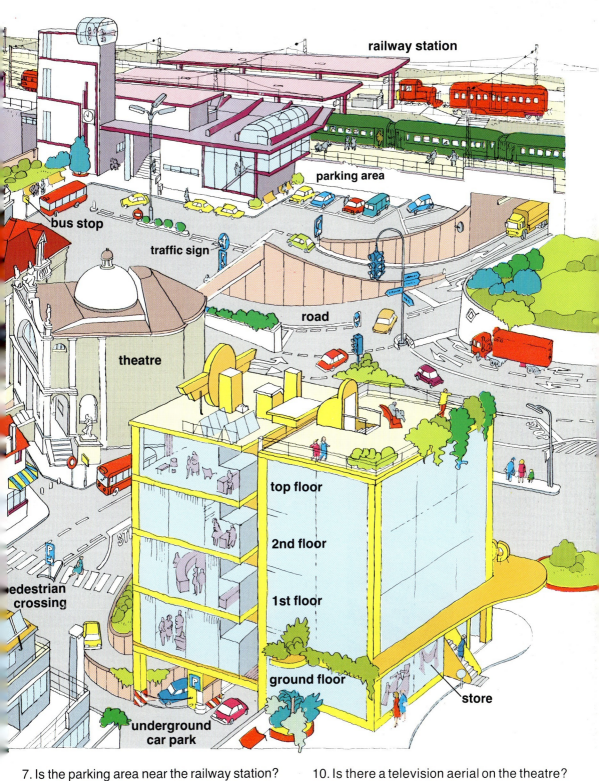

7. Is the parking area near the railway station?
   ....

8. Is the pedestrian crossing near the store?
   ....

9. Is the steeple on the Town Hall? ....

10. Is there a television aerial on the theatre?
    ....

to walk

to run

to photograph

to visit a museum

to wait

to meet

to park

to cross the road

to throw away

to post

A DAY IN TOWN

Study the picture on pages 10 and 11 and then complete the story. (Choose the words from the list below).

You can park your car in the .... area near the railway .... and walk into the centre of the .... There you can visit the Town .... and photograph the old .... and the .... with the steeple. If you .... the road at the .... crossing you arrive at a big store with four .... In the evening you can meet your .... at the .... After the show you can .... at the bus stop for a bus to the .... station where you parked your ....

- ☐ car ☐ church ☐ cross ☐ floors
- ☐ friends ☐ Hall ☐ parking
- ☐ pedestrian ☐ railway ☐ station
- ☐ theatre ☐ tower ☐ town ☐ wait

Follow the line from the Entrance to the Exit passing each drawing only once. Each time you come to a drawing write the name of the action it suggests. These actions are given in the correct order on the Solution Page.
the Solution Page.

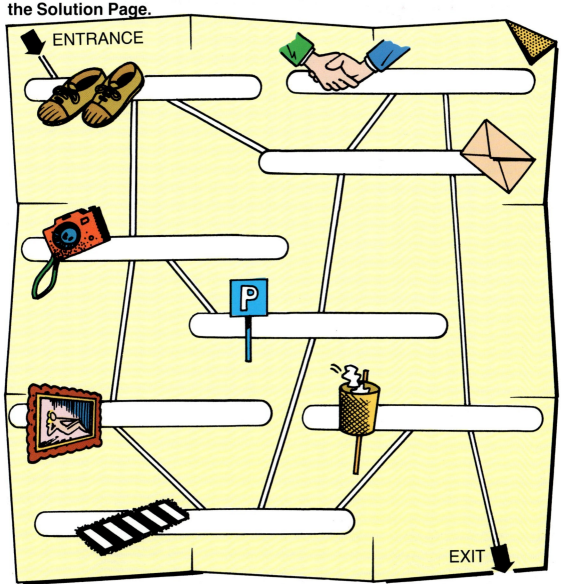

Fit the VERBS of the above game into che squares. Begin with the long verb that starts with letter P.

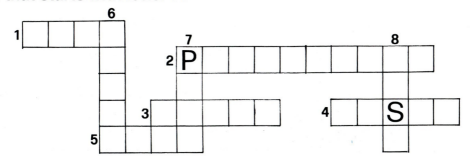

AN AIRPORT RAILWAY STATION

A
1. luggage trolley
2. porter
3. passenger
4. ticket collector
5. booking office
6. luggage lockers

B
1. suitcase
2. folding table
3. compartment
4. corridor

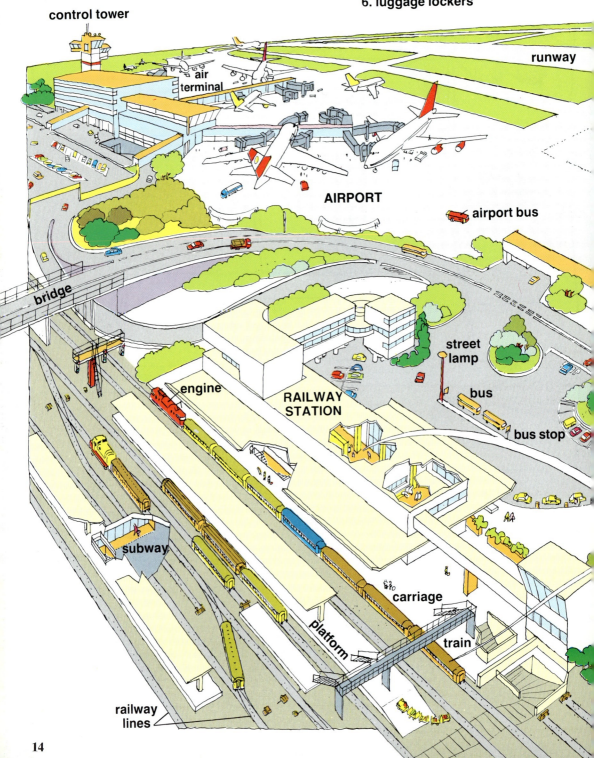

a passport

to pack

to leave

to arrive

to fly

to land

to travel

to wave

to get on   to get off

Fill in the missing letters or re-arrange the letters to form the names of things or people you can see at an airport or things you can see at a railway station.

AT THE AIRPORT

1. A _ _ _ P _ _ _ _
   W _ _ _
   W _ _ _ S _ _ _
   W _ _ _ _ W
   A _ _   _ E _ _ I _ A _

2. S H E S T O S   _____
   S R A D W E T   _____
   N A G H R A   _____
   Y A W N U R   _____
   R E D U R D   _____

AT THE RAILWAY STATION

3. S _ _ W _ _
   _ L _ T F _ _ _
   _ _ I _ W _ _ L _ _ E _
   _ R O _ _ _ Y
   C _ _ P _ _ T M _ _ _

4. R C A I R A E G   _____
   G E E N I N   _____
   G R E D I B   _____
   I N T R A   _____
   A U E L G G G   _____

Complete the story from the illustrations. You can find all the words in the pictures on pages 14, 15 and 16.

I packed my _____ and took

my _____. Then I travelled

by _____ to the

_____. I like

to look out of the _____

of the _____ and

the _____ is always very kind!

I'd like to be a _____

or work in the _____.

Oh no! I've forgotten my _____.

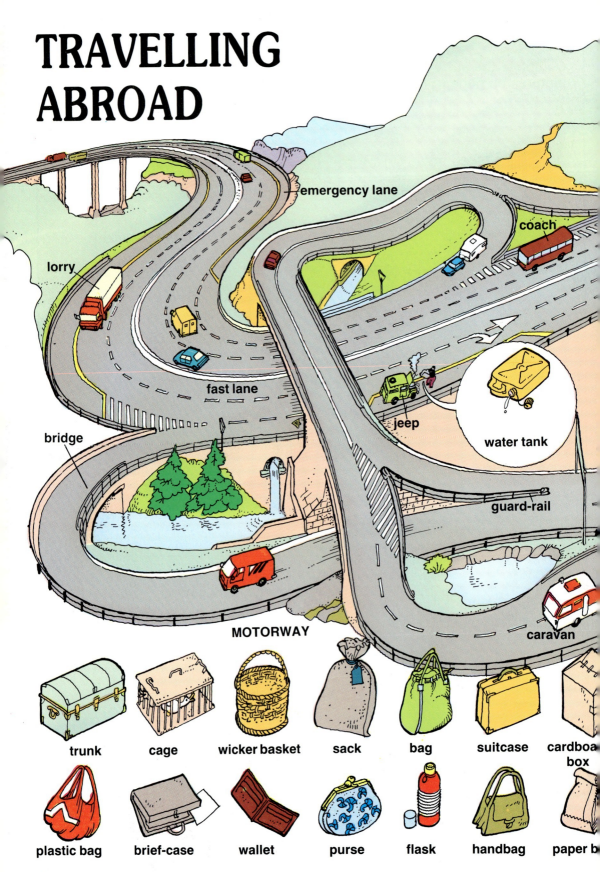

Can you re-write these mixed-up words correctly? Six of them are in the picture and six are illustrated on the left. Example: FIREB-SEAC ___BRIEF-CASE___

1. KNETAR _____
2. REITNORF _____
3. BIGRED _____
4. RYLRO _____
5. KCURT _____
6. YOMATROW _____
7. CAUSETIS _____
8. KNURT _____
9. HNBGADA _____
10. RUPES _____
11. STAKEB _____
12. LATLEW _____

19

to drive

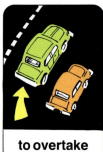
to overtake

to thumb a lift/to hitch-hike

to call a taxi

to take a bus

slow

fast

Read these sentences carefully and then say if they are TRUE or FALSE. If you don't know you can find the answers on the Solution Page.

TRUE FALSE

1. If you want to overtake another car on the motorway you must use the fast lane. ☐ ☐

2. You can park your car at the guard-rail. ☐ ☐

3. There are no bus stops on the motorway. ☐ ☐

4. When you cross the frontier you must stop at the customs. ☐ ☐

5. You can thumb a lift on the motorway. ☐ ☐

6. In Great Britain you drive on the right-hand side of the road. ☐ ☐

7. People can travel in a tanker ☐ ☐

8. You can call a taxi on the motorway. ☐ ☐

9. You can't take your camper or caravan on the motorway. ☐ ☐

10. Fast is the opposite of slow. ☐ ☐

**Read the list of words here below and then join the numbers in the drawing only if you can find the objects illustrated here.
What can you see in the picture? I can see _____.**

1. caravan
2. purse
3. wallet
4. flask
5. motorway
6. guard-rail
7. sack
8. camper
9. bridge
10. jeep
11. toll gate
12. wicker basket
13. cage
14. paper bag
15. traffic sign
16. suitcase
17. handbag
18. water tank
19. car
20. trailer truck
21. trunk
22. motor bike
23. cart
24. lorry
25. coach

PEOPLE AT WORK

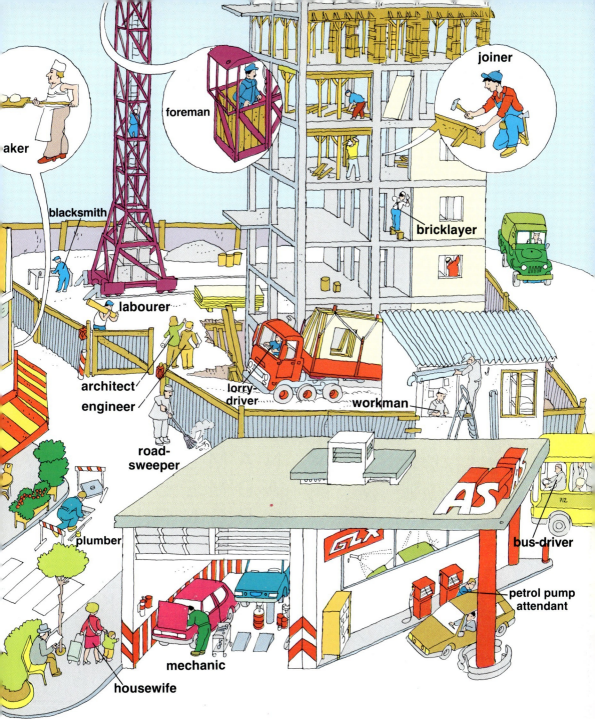

Complete the sentences. Fill in the correct action from the list at the side.

1. A shop-assistant _ _ _ _ _ things to people.
2. A petrol-pump attendant _ _ _ _ _ _ _ your car.
3. A bus-driver _ _ _ _ _ _ his bus.
4. A porter _ _ _ _ _ _ _ suitcases.
5. A secretary _ _ _ _ _ in an office.
6. A computer operator _ _ _ _ _ _ the keys on her computer.

| carries |
| drives |
| fills up |
| pushes |
| sells |
| works |

to work

to carry

to direct the traffic

to draw a plan

to sell

to buy

to repair

to fill up

to pull

to push

Find the names of the jobs in this list in the Letter Maze. Score them out as you find them. Then write the remaining letters in the spaces below and discover an old English saying.

- ☐ baker
- ☐ barman
- ☐ blacksmith
- ☐ clerk
- ☐ driver
- ☐ engineer
- ☐ foreman
- ☐ gardener
- ☐ joiner
- ☐ mechanic
- ☐ operator
- ☐ plumber
- ☐ typist
- ☐ workman

N	A	M	K	R	O	W	A	L	B
L	G	A	R	D	E	N	E	R	L
N	A	M	E	R	O	F	W	O	A
A	D	M	E	C	H	A	N	I	C
M	P	R	N	R	L	K	A	N	K
R	L	D	I	N	O	E	P	R	S
A	U	L	G	V	A	Y	R	E	M
B	M	M	N	A	E	K	E	K	I
S	B	J	E	A	C	R	K	A	T
R	E	N	I	O	J	A	D	B	H
U	R	O	T	A	R	E	P	O	L
L	B	T	S	I	P	Y	T	O	Y

___ ____ ___ __

____ _____ ____

__ ____ ___.

Follow the letters. Go from the name of a person to the object that represents his or her job. The letters spell what each person usually does. Then complete the sentences below.

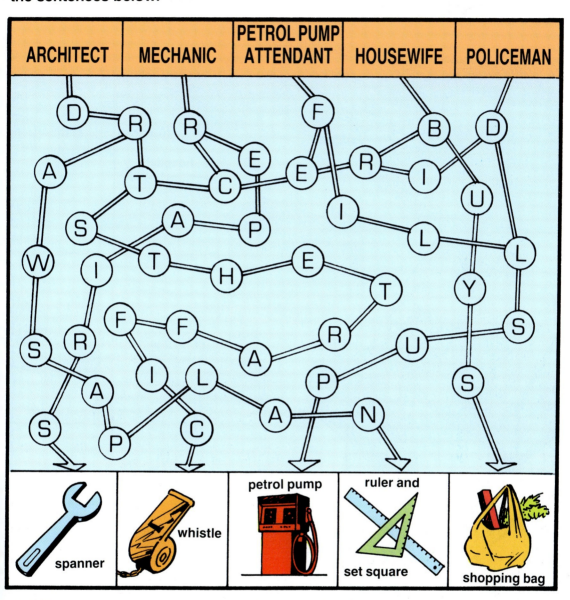

1. When an _ _ _ _ _ _ _ _ _ draws a plan he uses a set square and a _ _ _ _ _.
2. When a mechanic repairs a car, he sometimes uses a _ _ _ _ _ _ _.
3. You can fill up your car at a petrol _ _ _ _.
4. A _ _ _ _ _ _ _ _ _ buys food and carries it home in a shopping _ _ _.
5. When a _ _ _ _ _ _ _ _ _ directs the _ _ _ _ _ _ _ he sometimes uses a _ _ _ _ _ _ _.

25

Read these sentences carefully and then say if they are   TRUE   or   FALSE

1. People live in chalets in the centre of town.
2. There are many skyscrapers in the mountains.
3. A country cottage is a small detached house.
4. An attic is at the top of a building.
5. In town you can find many farms.
6. Castles always have large verandas.
7. People don't live on a terrace or balcony.

 small/big

 short/tall

 dirty/clean

 new/old

 tidy/untidy

 hot/cold

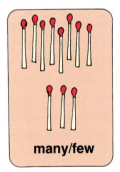 many/few

 narrow/wide

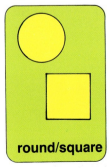 round/square

 light/dark

Fill in the crossword, using some of the words in the little vocabulary on the left.

Which five words, illustrated in the little vocabulary, are not included in the crossword?

1. ....
2. ....
3. ....
4. ....
5. ....

28

Fill in the missing letters. (All the words are in the picture on pages 26 and 27.) Then blacken the spaces in the drawing below only if the numbers correspond to one of the figures illustrated here. Write what appears in the drawing here. _____

1. T E R R A C E
2. B _ I _ D _ N _
3. H _ S _ I _ A _
4. C _ A _ E _
5. S _ I _ M _ N _ P _ O _
6. L _ K _
7. C _ S _ L _
8. G _ R _ G _
9. A _ T _ C
10. F _ R _
11. M _ T _ L
12. P _ R _ I _ G A _ E _
13. C _ M _ E _
14. S _ Y _ C _ A _ E _

THE HOUSE

Put the following objects in the correct rooms in the house.
☐ armchair ☐ back door ☐ bath ☐ bed
☐ bell ☐ carpet ☐ cooker ☐ fireplace
☐ door mat ☐ refrigerator ☐ rug
☐ shower ☐ sink ☐ sofa ☐ stairs
☐ toilet ☐ steps ☐ wardrobe

HALL   KITCHEN

....

....

....

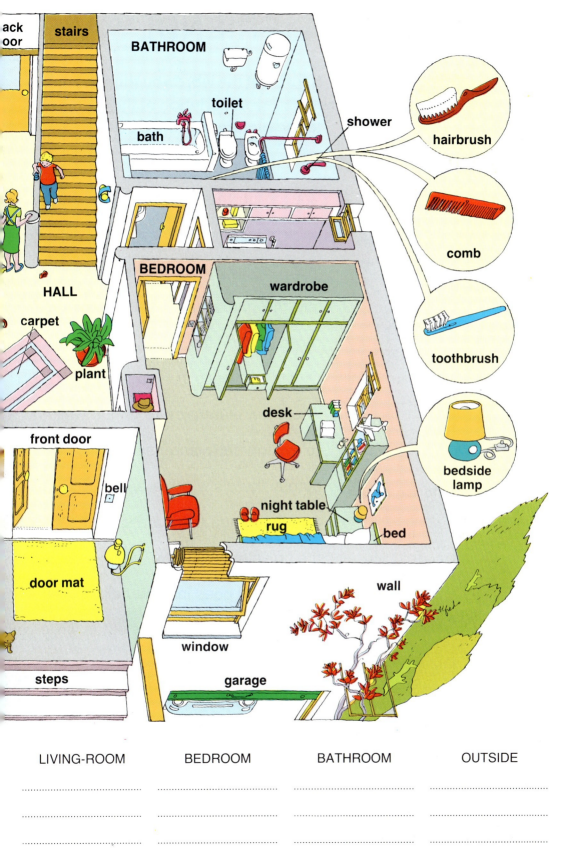

LIVING-ROOM	BEDROOM	BATHROOM	OUTSIDE
....	....	....	....
....	....	....	....
....	....	....	....

 roof
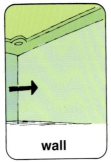 wall
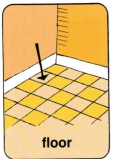 floor
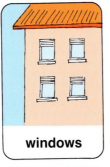 windows

A FRIENDLY VISIT

Score out the word you think is NOT correct. The description of the house refers to the picture on pages 30 and 31.

 shut/open
 to ring the bell

You go up the **stairs/steps** to the **front/back** door and **ring/wake** the bell. Your friend **opens/shuts** the door and you go into the **garden/hall**. In the hall there's a **rug/carpet** on the floor.

On the left there's the **living-room/bedroom**. There's a **plant/picture** on the wall and a **television set/piano** near the sofa. In one corner there's a table and some **chairs/armchairs** and there are some curtains at the **fire-place/window**.

 to go to bed
 to wake up

Your friend goes into the **hall/kitchen** and makes you a **cup/saucer** of tea while you go into the **bathroom/bedroom** to **wall/wash** your hands.

You and your friend walk in the **garage/garden** before you say "Goodbye".

 to get up
 to wash

The five objects illustrated above are hidden in the picture. Find them and then complete the sentences below.

1. The _ _ _ _ is under the _____
2. The _ _ _ is near the _____
3. The _ _ _ _ is above the _____
4. The _ _ _ _ _ _ _ _ _ is between the _____ and the _____
5. The _ _ _ _ _ _ _ _ _ _ is under the _____

corkscrew

cook

food

oil **vinegar**

cruet set

napkin

customer **waiter** **waitress**

fruit

fruit salad

cake

coffee

Answer the questions.

How many people are in the queue for food?
....
What has the waitress got in her hands?
....
What has the man at the cash-desk got in his hand?
....
How many people are sitting at the table?
....
How many chairs are there in the snack-bar?
....
How many of the following objects are on the table: napkin, plates, fork, knife, cake, cruet set, bread, glasses? ....

to cook

to eat

to chew

to drink

to cut

to pour

to serve

to diet

to be hungry

to be thirsty

Are these statements RIGHT or WRONG?

	RIGHT	WRONG
1. The usual place to cook is the living-room	☐	☐
2. You can have lunch in a snack-bar	☐	☐
3. If you are hungry you drink a large cup of coffee	☐	☐
4. You cut bread with a spoon	☐	☐
5. You can't chew a can	☐	☐
6. You can pour water from a jug into a glass	☐	☐
7. Waiters and waitresses can serve people in a snack-bar	☐	☐
8. You eat something if you are thirsty	☐	☐
9. You eat something if you are hungry	☐	☐
10. If you are dieting you can eat a lot of cake every day	☐	☐

What's the difference? Complete the names of what's missing in the picture on the right.

C☐☐☐-R☐☐☐☐☐☐☐☐ G☐☐☐☐

A B☐☐☐☐ roll M☐☐☐

C☐☐☐☐ S☐☐ N☐☐☐☐☐

W☐☐☐☐☐ S☐☐☐

K☐☐☐☐ F☐☐☐

How many are there in the picture? Answer in a sentence.

1. How many people are there? *There are* ....
2. How many of them are women? .... *of them are* ....
3. How many of them are men? ....
4. How many of them are children? *Only* .... *of them is a child*
5. How many cashiers are there? ....
6. How many trolleys are there? ....
7. How many assistants are there? *There's* ....

baker's

confec-
tioner's

fruiterer's/
fruit shop

fish monger's/
fish shop

butcher's

florist's/
flower shop

newspaper
kiosk

chemist's

dress shop

bookseller's/
bookshop

Re-arrange the names of these shop-keepers. Then find the letters indicated and re-write them in the spaces below. This gives you the name of the shop where you can buy a variety of food, such as, tea, coffee, rice, bread, sugar, oil and so on.

1. KAREB   _ _ _ _ _
            the 2nd

2. SHONFIMREG
   _ _ _ _ _ _ _ _ _ _
            the 8th

3. TRIFRUERE   _ _ _ _ _ _ _ _ _
                        the 7th

4. SITLOFR   _ _ _ _ _ _ _
                the 3rd

5. CNETOEOFCRIN
   _ _ _ _ _ _ _ _ _ _ _ _
   the 1st

6. KOSBELEORL
   _ _ _ _ _ _ _ _ _ _
            the 6th

7. RTHUBEC   _ _ _ _ _ _ _
                    the 7th

8. MESCITH   _ _ _ _ _ _ _
                    the 6th

☐   ☐☐☐☐☐'☐

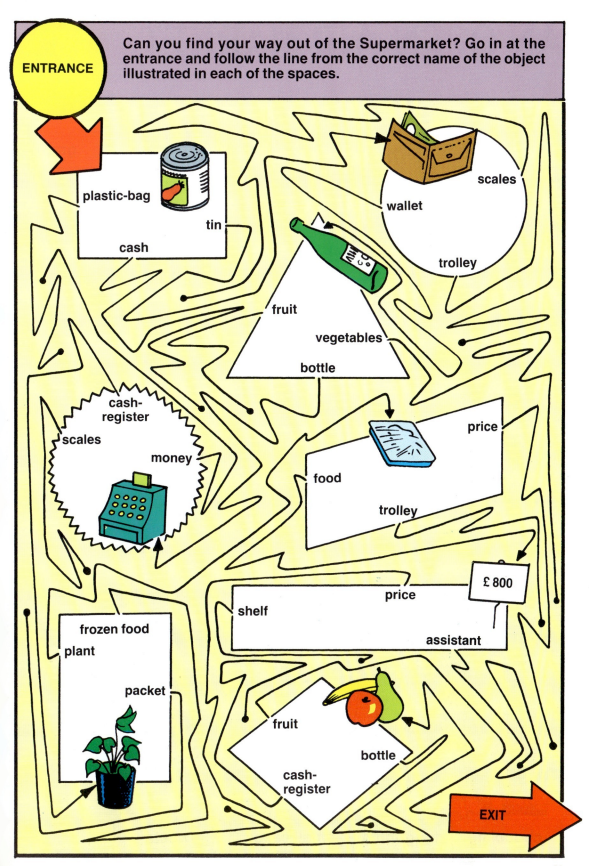

AN OPEN-AIR MARKET

VEGETABLE STALL

- lettuce
- carrots
- tomatoes
- onions
- courgettes
- peppers
- potatoes
- fennel
- garlic
- peas
- cabbages
- aubergines/eggplants
- broad beans
- pumpkin
- sole
- octopus
- eel
- ham
- crayfish
- cuttlefish
- perch
- salame
- scales
- sausages

PORK PRODUCTS STALL

SH STALL

PERSONAL NOTES: Complete with your own favourites.

FOOD I DON'T LIKE

My favourite fruit is ....

My favourite vegetable is ....

My favourite sweet is ....

My favourite fish is ....

My favourite pork product is ....

43

AT THE OPEN-AIR MARKET

Choose the correct word. Score out the incorrect ones.

1. **They are small and red:**
☐ a) cakes
☐ b) eels
☐ c) cherries

2. **You weigh them at the vegetable stall:**
☐ a) grapes
☐ b) carrots
☐ c) chocolates

3. **"Dear" means you have to pay**
☐ a) a lot
☐ b) a little
☐ c) a few

4. **You buy it at the fish stall:**
☐ a) a peach
☐ b) a pepper
☐ c) a perch

5. **It doesn't grow on a tree:**
☐ a) a pear
☐ b) a pineapple
☐ c) a strawberry

6. **It can be fresh or frozen:**
☐ a) bread
☐ b) fish
☐ c) salame

7. **You generally wrap it up:**
☐ a) a box of chocolates
☐ b) a bag of chestnuts
☐ c) a purse

8. **The stall-keeper at the confectionary stall can give you:**
☐ a) onions
☐ b) sausages
☐ c) doughnuts

In the list of letters below score out the names of the thirteen things you see in the illustration. Re-arrange the remaining letters to form the name of one of the stalls illustrated on pages 42 and 43.

C P E A R O C A R R O T N E E L F L E M O N S E S W E E T S C O C T O

P U S T I S A U S A G E S O C A K E N C H E R R I E S A A U B E R G I

N E R S A L A M E Y I C E - C R E A M

The name of the stall is ....

ODD ONE OUT
Underline the word you think has nothing in common with the other two.

1. book   dictionary   bookshelves

2. copy-book   teacher   blackboard

3. waste-paper basket   poster   calendar

4. map   poster   pupil

5. girl   boy   clothes-peg

6. school-bag   desk   chair

7. teacher   classroom   janitor

8. calendar   pen   chalk

Fill in the crossword from the following clues.

1 *Down.* It's in a school and has four walls, a door and a window.
1 *Across.* It's full of dates.
2. A boy or girl who goes to school.
3. You write with it.
4. The teacher writes on it for the class.
5. You may have one on a wall at school or at home.
6. You have a school one for your books.
7. Pupils write in this.
8. You put waste-paper in it.
9. The "opposite" of girl.
10. Pupils sit at one in the classroom.
11. He works in a school.
12. The teacher sits on one in the classroom.
13. The opposite of easy.

to read

to write

to talk or speak

to think

to listen (to)

to study

to look (at)

to draw

easy

difficult

Who is saying what? Choose from the sentences below and re-write them in the balloons:

1. "I don't want to study."
2. "I want to read this book."
3. "That's a map of South America."
4. "Listen to that bird!"
5. "I like drawing"
6. "Don't write on my copybook!"
7. "Answer my question!"
8. "It's time for school to begin."

Now write the number of the sentence opposite each letter and check your answers from the Solution Page.

A. __ B. __ C. __ D. __ E. __ F. __ G. __ H. __

IN THE OFFICE

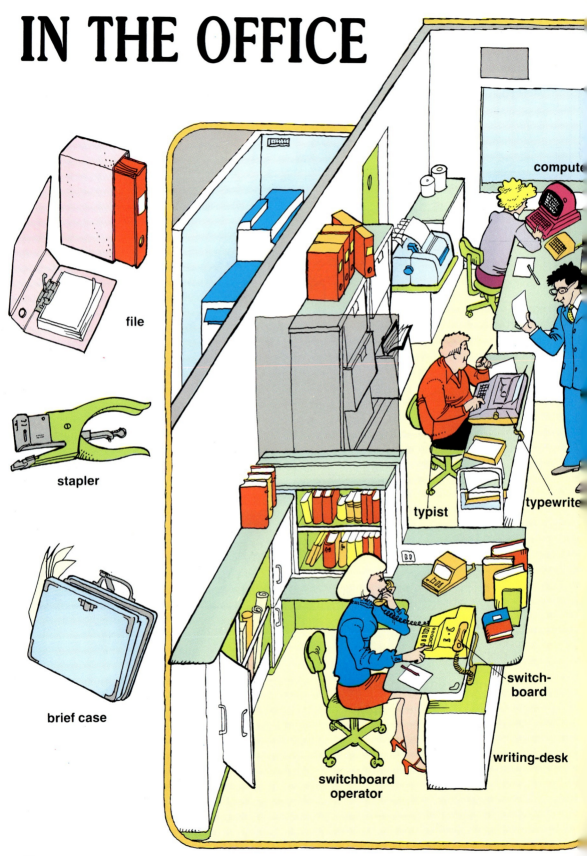

1. The secretary on the left is operating the _ w _ _ _ _ b _ _ _ _.
2. Another secretary is using a _ _ _ _ u _ _ _.
3. The _ _ n _ _ _ _ is looking at his notebook.
4. An _ _ _ _ c _ - _ _ _ is leaving the room.
5. There are a lot of f _ _ _ s in this office.
6. The _ y _ _ _ _ and the _ _ _ _ k are talking.
7. There is a p _ _ _ _ c _ _ _ _ _ _ near the door.

to be on time

to be late

to introduce

to dial

to type

to be tired

to sit down

to stand

to go

to come

IN THE OFFICE

Fill in the missing words from the list below.

1. The manager is .... the new clerk, Mr Brown.

2. "Telephone at once! .... four, five, o, nine, seven."

3. The typist .... to the office by bus.

4. "The manager's telephoning at the moment. Please .... down.

5. I've worked all morning and I .... very ....

6. The switchboard operator always arrives exactly at nine o'clock. She .... always ....

7. Everyone .... home in the evening.

8. "It's ten past nine! You ....

9. The clerk is .... near the photocopier because he wants to make a copy of a letter.

10. "These letters are urgent. .... them at once, please."

☐ is...on time ☐ 're late ☐ introducing
☐ dial ☐ type ☐ 'm...tired ☐ sit
☐ standing ☐ goes ☐ comes

Score out the names of the above objects in this "list" of letters. The remaining letters give you the name of someone who works in an office. Write the name in the sentence below.

S T E L E P H O N E E P H O T O C O P I E R C

C A R D I N D E X R B R I E F C A S E E S T A

P L E R T A C A L C U L A T O R R F I L E Y D E

S K D I A R Y

A _ _ _ _ _ _ _ _ _ _ _ works in an office.

A FASHION - SHOW

Choose the right word. Score out the two wrong articles of clothing.

1. With jeans you can wear a { shirt / skirt / suit

2. Over a dress you can put on { sandals / trousers / a coat

3. When it's cold you wear a { shirt / blouse / wind-cheater

4. With a skirt you can wear a { T-shirt / dress / suit

5. When it's warm you wear a { woollen jacket / sweater / blouse

6. Men wear { a skirt and jumper / a jacket and trousers / a dress and silk scarf

7. On your feet you wear { shoes / hats / ties

8. On your head you can wear { a leather jacket / a T-shirt / a silk scarf

silk

wool

cotton

leather

cloth

zip

buttons

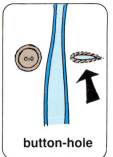
button-hole

to put on

to take off

SPELLING TEST: In this list seven words are misspelt. Write the correct spelling at the side.

leather ....
shoes ....
sweter ....
sute ....
buttons ....
button-whole ....
skirt ....
boots ....
wollen ....
trouser ....
jumper ....
jacket ....
raincoat ....
shirt ....
blouse ....
dres ....
sandals ....
coton ....
scarf ....
tie ....

Find the 8 words beginning with "S" on pages 54 and 55.

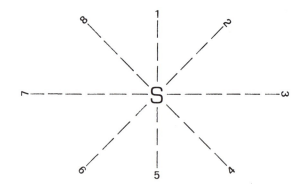

Compare these figures with the ones on pages 54 and 55. Write the names of the two articles of clothing that are missing on each figure in the squares.

A. ☐☐☐☐-☐☐☐☐☐☐☐/
   ☐☐☐☐☐

B. ☐☐☐☐☐☐☐☐☐/☐☐☐☐☐

C. ☐☐☐/☐☐☐☐

D. ☐☐☐☐☐☐/☐☐☐☐☐☐☐☐☐

E. ☐☐☐☐ ☐☐☐☐☐/
   ☐☐☐☐☐☐☐ ☐☐☐☐☐☐

F. ☐☐☐☐☐/☐☐☐

HERE and THERE

From the list on the right choose the opposites of these words and write them in the space provided

far -	near	at the back
on -		down
off -		near
up -		on
with -		outside
inside -		under
at the front -		without

Fit the remaining prepositions into the squares

It's one o'clock

...five past two

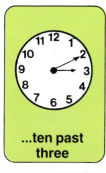
...ten past three

...a quarter past four

...twenty past five

...half past six

...twenty to seven

...a quarter to eight

...ten to nine

...five to ten

GEORGE'S DAY

Complete the game on the opposite page and then write the story.

Begin: *Every day George gets up at half past seven.* Here are some words to help you: *has, in the morning, goes, house, in an office, snack-bar, in the afternoon, in the evening, is sleeping, all night.*

Look at the vocabulary on this page and say whether these sentences are true or false.

	TRUE	FALSE
1. The mountain climber is carrying an ice-axe	☐	☐
2. The snowman is wearing a wind-cheater	☐	☐
3. The Saint Bernard dog isn't pulling a sleigh	☐	☐
4. Some skiers are using the ski lift	☐	☐
5. There's a mountain hut near the ice-rink	☐	☐
6. The instructor isn't wearing a cap and scarf	☐	☐

to ski

to skate

to fall

to slip

to help

to be cold

to shiver

to get warm

to sneeze

to snow

Fill in the missing letters. All the words begin with the letter "S". You can find them in the picture on pages 62 and 63 or in the little vocabulary on this page.

				S				
1								
2				S				
3		N						
4				P				
5		L						
6				R				
7			I		R			
8		K						
9		T				S		
10			E					
11				D				
12		H						
13				Z				
14							N	
15				B				

GUESS WHAT!

My first syllable is something white and cold.

My second syllable is the opposite of woman.

My whole is fun to make with gloves on.

I'm a _ _ _ _ _ _ _ _!

Fill in the spaces only if the numbers correspond with the names of the drawings here at the side.

1. sledge
2. chair lift
3. cable-way
4. snowballs
5. fir tree
6. ski cap
7. ice-axe
8. skier
9. snowman
10. mountain climber
11. ski sticks
12. scarf
13. ski boots
14. mountain hut
15. gloves
16. skis

In the picture there is

....

a wing

a beak

a claw

ears

tails

a trunk

a mane

horns

whiskers

hoofs

The drawer of these 12 animals made an error in 10 of them. Here below write the ten names and the drawer's errors and then the names of the two correctly-drawn animals. The names of the different parts of the animals are here at the side.

ANIMALS   ERRORS

1. ....
2. ....
3. ....
4. ....
5. ....
6. ....
7. ....
8. ....
9. ....
10. ....

The two correctly-drawn animals are the .... and the ....

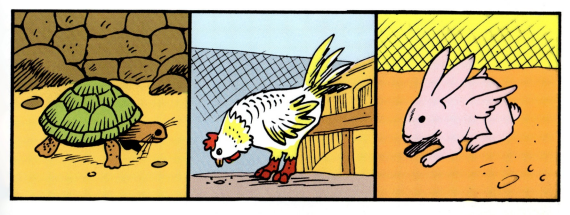

You can find these animals in the picture. Write their names at the side.

1. It's a bird but it can't fly
2. It has a trunk
3. It has a long neck
4. It crawls along the ground
5. It can change its colour
6. It has a black and white striped skin
7. It's very graceful and can run fast
8. It lives in the desert

to dive

to swim

to jump

to hide

to crawl

to chase

to sniff

to scratch

to swing

to feed

Look for these verbs in the letter maze. Score them out as you find them. Then fill in the missing spaces below with the remaining letters.

- ☐ chase
- ☐ crawl
- ☐ dive
- ☐ feed
- ☐ hide
- ☐ jump
- ☐ scratch
- ☐ sniff
- ☐ swim
- ☐ swing

L	S	A	P	N	I	M	A
D	W	C	L	M	I	W	S
B	I	A	R	E	U	K	N
I	N	V	R	A	N	J	I
D	G	T	E	C	T	O	F
T	H	E	S	A	H	C	F
E	M	F	E	E	D	I	H

☐☐☐☐☐☐[S] can't speak, so ☐☐ ☐☐☐☐ ☐☐ ☐☐☐☐

An elephant story: I was travelling to London by train the other day. In the compartment, opposite me, a man was making little balls of newspaper and throwing them out of the window.
"Why are you doing that?" I asked.
"To keep the elephants away*", he replied.
"But there aren't any elephants in this country", I said.
"That's why!" The man answered.

*Keep the elephants away = not permit the elephants to come.

Can you name the nine different animals that make up this strange creature? Write the names in the spaces below.

1. B _ _ _ _ _ _
2. F _ _ _ _ _ _ _
3. G _ _ _ _ _ _
4. Z _ _ _ _
5. D _ _ _ _ _ _ _ _
6. O _ _ _ _ _ _
7. C _ _ _ _ _ _ _ _
8. C _ _ _ _ _ _ _ _
9. E _ _ _ _ _ _ _

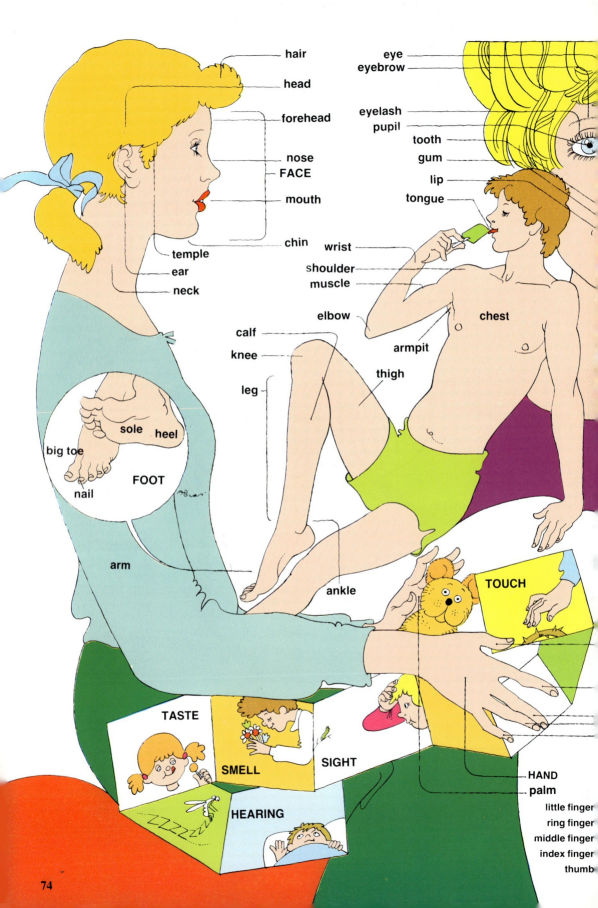

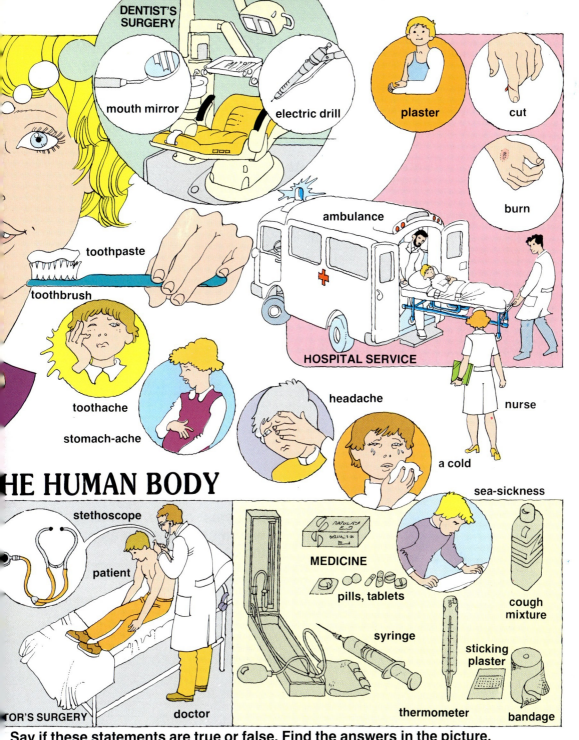

Say if these statements are true or false. Find the answers in the picture.

                                                                                  TRUE   **FALSE**

1. A dentist uses a mouth mirror
2. The wrist is part of the arm
3. If you have a cut on your finger you put a tablet on it
4. You use a sticking plaster for your nose if you have a cold
5. The temple is part of the hand
6. The heel is part of the foot

fat/thin

handsome/ugly

strong/weak

tall/short

fair/dark

straight/curly

right/left

happy/sad

young/old

long/short

OPPOSITES Write the opposites of these adjectives in the squares.

long ☐☐☐☐☐

curly ☐☐☐☐☐☐☐☐

happy ☐☐☐

tall ☐☐☐☐☐

old ☐☐☐☐☐

handsome ☐☐☐☐

thin ☐☐☐

dark ☐☐☐☐

strong ☐☐☐☐

left ☐☐☐☐☐

Find the names of the following things. They have the same names as parts of the human body.

1. A young cow ☐☐☐☐

2. A tropical tree ☐☐☐☐

3. A boy or girl who goes to school ☐☐☐☐☐

4. Another name for "language" ☐☐☐☐☐☐

5. A piece of furniture with drawers ☐☐☐☐☐

6. Guns and pistols are this ☐☐☐☐

7. A needle has one ☐☐☐

Here below write the names of the parts of the body in the 15 drawings. Put them in order from the top (hair) to the bottom (foot).

1. H A I R
2. _ _ _ _ _ _ _ _
3. _ _ _
4. _ _ _ _
5. _ _ _ _ _
6. _ _ _ _
7. _ _ _ _
8. _ _ _ _ _ _ _ _ _
9. _ _ _ _ _
10. _ _ _ _
11. _ _ _ _ _
12. _ _ _ _
13. _ _ _ _
14. _ _ _ _ _
15. F O O T

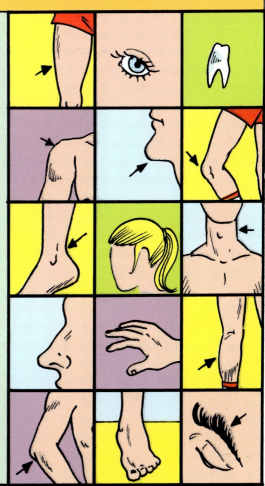

Find the FOUR suitable adjectives from the list below to describe this man.

handsome - thin - strong - ugly
short - fat - weak - tall

1. .... 2. ....
3. .... 4. ....

Find a suitable object in the picture for the following sports.

(a) boxing .... (b) diving .... (c) fencing ....
(d) football .... (e) gymnastics .... (f) hockey ....
(g) rowing .... (h) tennis .... (i) swimming ....

KEEP FIT - PRACTISE SPORTS
Fill in the missing words from the list below.

Practise ....! It's good for your health. It strengthens your .... and keeps your body ....

You can do .... every morning, bend and stretch in your bedroom near an .... window or throw and .... a ball with your friends in a park or ....

You can play football: .... the ball makes your knees .... and if you are the goal-keeper and .... a lot of goals you strengthen your ....

Other good exercises are lifting weights and .... but it's best to do these sports with a ....

☐ arms ☐ catch ☐ coach ☐ exercises ☐ fit

☐ garden ☐ kicking ☐ muscles ☐ open

☐ save ☐ shooting ☐ sports ☐ strong

Here are 10 symbols of different sports. Beside each one you'll find its name, but you must put the letters in their right order. Then look at the squares below where the names of the 10 sports are written. In each square write the letter you can see in the symbol that corresponds to that sport, and you will be able to read the name of a modern Olympic Games contest.

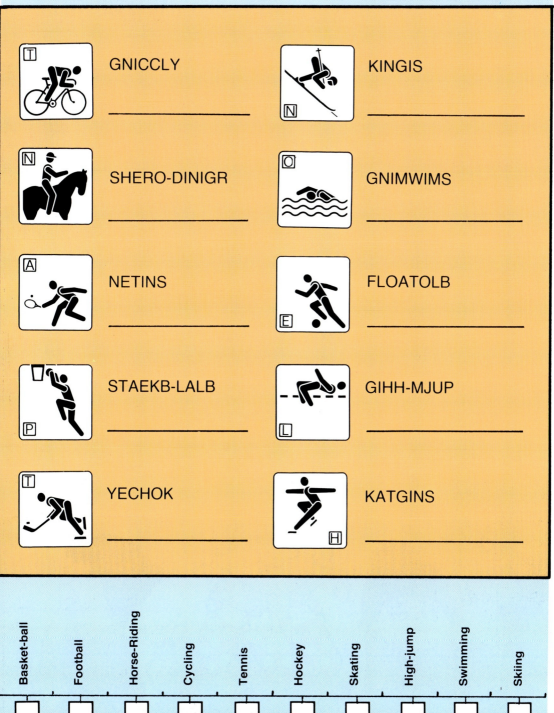

Fill in the names of some of the things, illustrated here, that you can do during the summer holidays.

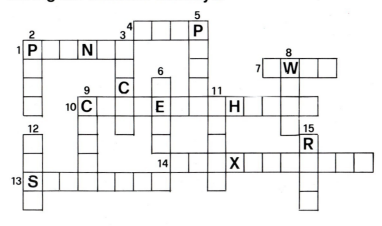

sunrise

sunset

WORD ASSOCIATION

Beside each word on the left write a word from the list on the right that is connected with it. Use each word only once.

day/night

sun

moon

stars

clouds (cloudy)

sea

deck-chair

beach umbrella

sea	*island*	aeroplane
church	....	baby-sitter
runway	....	button-hole
cart	....	cashier
baby	....	diving
building	....	floors
bath	....	food
snack bar	....	gloves
checkout	....	holidays
fruit	....	horse
school	....	island ✓
typist	....	sheep
boots	....	shoes
button	....	sleigh
snow	....	smell
lamb	....	sponge
swimming	....	steeple
nose	....	teacher
boxing	....	typewriter
summer	....	vegetables

The pictures will help you complete this story: fill in the missing letters and rearrange the jumbled words.

In summer the ☀ s_ _ _ is

w r a m _ _ _ _. It's fun to

_ _ _ _ _ near the

s _ a. You can i f h s _ _ _ _,

_ _ _ _ _ _ _ _ _ and

i m w s _ _ _ _ from 🌅 _ _ _ _ _ _ _

to t u s s n e _ _ _ _ _ _. If it's a

☁ _ _ _ _ _ day you can

t e l n i s _ _ _ _ _ _ to music or r _ a _ a book.

You can s _ e _ p under the ⭐ _ _ _ _ _

by the light of the 🌙 _ _ _ _

and in the m _ r _ i _ g you can k w e a _ _ _ _ _

up to the singing of the 🐦 _ _ _ _ _.

Wordlist

This is an alphabetical list of all the words illustrated in this book. By each word you will find the number of the page(s) containing the illustration(s) of that word. If there are any words you can't remember, then look them up on the page(s) where they are illustrated.

A
aeroplane 15
African animals 70
air terminal 14
airport 14
airport bus 14
along 58
ambulance 75
animals 66
ankle 74
antelope 70
apples 42
architect 23
arm 74
armchair 30
armpit 74
arrive (to) 16
articulated lorry 19
assistant 39
at the back 58
at the front 58
attic 26

B
baby-sitter 22
back door 31
bag 18, 39
baker 23, 40
balcony 26
bananas 42
bandage 75
barman 22
basket-ball 79
bath 31
bathroom 31
bay 6
be cold (to) 64
be hungry (to) 36
be late (to) 52
be on time (to) 52
be thirsty (to) 36
be tired (to) 52
beach 6
beach umbrella 84
beak 68
bed 31
bedroom 31
bedside lamp 31
bee 67
bell 31, 32
bend (to) 80
between 58

big 28
big toe 74
bird 67
black 8
blackboard 46
blacksmith 23
blouse 55
blue 8
booking office 14
books 46
bookseller's 40
bookshelves 30, 46
bookshop 40
boots 54
bottles 39
boxing 79
boy 46
bread 34, 42
bricklayer 23
bridge 14, 18, 59
brief-case 18, 50
broad beans 43
brown 8
buffalo 70
buildings 26
bull 67
burn 75
bus 14
bus stop 11, 14
bus-driver 23
bushes 7
butcher's 40
button-hole 56
buttons 56
buy (to) 24

C
cabbages 43
cable-way 62
cage 18, 58
cakes 35, 42
calculator 51
calendar 46
calf 67, 74
call a taxi (not) 20
camp (to) 82
camper 19, 27
can 34
canary 66
car 19, 27
car park 14
caravan 18, 27

card index 51
cardboard box 18
carpet 31
carriage 14
carrots 43
carry (to) 24
cart 19
cash-desk 34
cash-register 34
cashier 22, 38
castle 27
cat 66
catch (to) 80
cemetery 10
chair 30, 34, 46
chair lift 63
chalet 27
chalk 46
chameleon 71
change 34
chase (to) 72
cheap 44
checkout 38
cheetah 70
chemist's 40
cherries 42
chest 74
chestnuts 42
chew (to) 36
chick 67
chimney pot 58
chin 74
chocolate 42
church 10
claw 68
clean 28
clerk 22, 50
climb (to) 82
climbing-irons 62
cloth 56
clothes-peg 46
clouds 7, 84
cloudy 84
coach 18, 79
coast 7
coat 55
cock 67
coffee 35
cold 28, 75
collect (to) 82
comb 31
come (to) 52

compartment 14
computer 50
computer operator 22
confectionary stall 42
confectioner's 40
control tower 14
cook (to) 36
cook 22, 35
cooker 30
copy-book 47
corkscrew 35
corridor 14
cotton 56
cough mixture 75
counter 39
country 27
country cottage 26
country road 6
courgettes 43
court 78
cow 67
cow's horns 58
crane 70
crawl 72
crayfish 43
crocodile 71
cross (to) the road 12
cruet set 35
cultivated field 6
cup 30
cupboard 30
curly 76
curtain 30
customers 35, 39
customs 19
cut (to) 36, 75
cuttlefish 43
cycle (to) 83
cycling 78
cyclist 78

D
dark 28, 76
day 84
dear 44
deck-chair 84
dentist 75
desk 31, 47
desk diary 51
dial (to) 52
dictionary 46
diet (to) 36

difficult 48
direct the traffic (to) 24
dirty 28
dive (to) 72
diver 79
diving-boards 79
do exercises (to) 80, 83
doctor 75
doctor's surgery 75
dog 66
donkey 67
door mat 31
doughnuts 42
down 58
draw (to) 24, 48
dress 54
dress shop 40
drink (to) 36
drinks 38
drive (to) 20
dromedary 70
duck 67

E
ears 68, 74
easy 48
eat (to) 36
eel 43
elbow 74
electric drill 75
electrician 22
elephant 71
emergency lane 18
engine 14
engineer 23
entrance 38
exit 38
eye 74
eyebrow 74
eyelash 74

F
face 74
fair 76
fall (to) 64
far 58
farm 27, 66
fast 20
fast lane 18
fat 76
feed (to) 72
fence 59
fencing 78
fennel 43
few 28
field 78
figs 42
file 50

fill up (to) 24
filling-station 10
fir-trees 62
fire engine 15
fire-place 30
first floor 11
fish (to) 83
fishmonger's 40
fish shop 40
fish stall 43
flamingo 71
flask 18
flat 26
floors 26, 32
florist's 40
flower shop 40
flowers 6
fly (to) 16
folding table 14
food 35, 39
foot 74
football 78
footballers 78
forehead 74
foreman 23
fork 34
freezer 39
fresh 44
front door 31
frontier 19
frozen 39, 44
fruit 35, 39
fruit salad 35
fruit shop 40
fruit stall 42
fruiterer's 40

G
garage 27, 31
garden 30
gardener 22
garlic 43
gazelle 70
get off (to) 16, 59
get on (to) 16, 58
get up (to) 32
get warm (to) 64
giraffe 70
girl 46
give (to) 44
glasses 34
globe 47
gloves 62
go (to) 52
go to bed (to) 32
goal 78
goalkeeper 78
goat 67

goldfish 66
goods train 15
goose 67
gorilla 71
grapes 42
green 8
grey 8
ground floor 11
guard-rail 18
guinea pig 67
guitar 83
gum 74
gymnastics 78

H
hair 74
hairbrush 31
hall 31
ham 43
hamster 66
hand 74
handbag 18
handsome 76
hangar 15
happy 76
hat 54
head 74
headache 75
hearing 74
hedge 6
heel 74
help (to) 64
hen 67
here 58
heron 70
hide (to) 72
high-jump 79
hill 6
hippopotamus 71
hoofs 68
horizon 7
horns 68
horse 19
horse-riding 78
horseman 78
hospital 26
hospital service 75
hostess 15
hot 28
hotel 27
horse 67
house 10, 30
housewife 23
hurdling 79
hyena 70

I
ice-axe 62

ice-cream 42
ice-hockey 79
ice-rink 56, 79
ice-skating 79
in 58
index finger 74
inside 58
introduce 52
islands 7

J
jackal 70
jacket 54
jam 42
janitor 46
jeep 18
jeans 55
joiner 23
judo 79
jump (to) 72
jumper 55
jumping 78

K
kick (to) 80
kitchen 30
kitten 66
knee 74
knife 34

L
labourer 23
lake 6, 27
lamb 67
lamp 30
land 16
large detached house 2
leather 54, 56
leave (to) 16
leaves 6
left 76
leg 74
lemons 42
leopard 71
lettuce 43
level-crossing 58
lift (to) 80
light 28
light blue 8
lion 70
lip 74
listen (to) 48, 82
little (a) 44
little finger 74
living-room 30
lollipops 42
long 76
look at (to) 48

lorry 15, 18
lorry-driver 23
lot 44
luggage 58
luggage lockers 14
luggage trolley 14

M
manager 22, 51
mane 68
many 28
map 46
meadow 6
meat 38
mechanic 23
medicine 75
meet (to) 12
melon 42
menu 34
middle finger 74
money 34, 38
monkey 71
moon 84
motel 27
motorbike 19
motorway 18
mountain 6
mountain chain 63
mountain climber 62
mountain hut 62
mountains 27
mouse 67
mouth 74
mouth mirror 74
muscle 74
museum 12
music 82

N
nail 74
napkin 35
narrow 28
nature 6
near 58
neck 74
net 78
new 28
news-stand 10
newspaper kiosk 10, 40
night 84
night table 31
nose 74
nurse 75

O
oar 79
octopus 43
off 58

office 50
office-boy 22, 51
oil 35
old 28, 76
on 58
onions 43
open 32
open-air market 42
oranges 42
ostrich 70
outside 58
overtake (to) 20
ox 67

P
pack (to) 16
packets 38
paint (to) 83
palm (hand) 74
paper bag 18
parcel 58
park (to) 12
parking area 11, 27
parrot 66
passenger 14
passport 16
patient 75
pavement 10, 58
pay (to) 44
peaches 42
peak 6, 63
peas 43
pedestrian crossing 11
pen 46
people 22
peppers 43
perch 43
petrol pump attendant 23
pets 66
photocopier 51
photograph (to) 12
photographs 82
piano 30
picture 30
pig 67
pigeon 67
pills 75
pilot 15
pineapple 42
pink 8
plain 7
plan 24
plants 31, 38
plaster 75
plastic bag 18, 38
plates 34
platform 14
play (to) 83
plumber 23

policeman 22
pond 7
pork products stall 43
porter 14, 22
post (to) 12
poster 47
postman 22
potatoes 43
pour (to) 36
price 39
pull (to) 24, 80
pupil 46, 74
puppy 66
purple 8
purse 18, 38
push (to) 24
put on (to) 56

Q
queue 34

R
rabbit 67
race-track 78
railway lines 14
railway station 11, 14
raincoat 54
ranch 26
read (to) 48, 83
red 8
refrigerator 30
repair (to) 24
rhinoceros 71
ride (to) 82
right 76
ring 78
ring finger 74
ring (to) 32
river 7
road 11
road-sweeper 23
rocks 6
roller-skating 78
roof 26, 32
round 28, 58
row (to) 83
rowing 79
rudder 15
rug 31
run (to) 12
runner 78
running 78
runway 14

S
sack 18
sad 76
sail 79

sailing 79
sailing-boat 79
Saint Bernard dog 62
salame 43
sandals 55
saucer 30
sausages 43
save (to) 80
scales 43
scarf 54, 55
school 10
schoolbag 47
scratch (to) 72
sea 7, 84
sea-sickness 75
second floor 11
secretary 22, 50
sell (to) 24
serve (to) 36
sheep 67
shelf 39
shells 82
shirt 55
shiver (to) 64
shoes 54
shoot (to) 80
shop 10
shop window 10
shop-assistant 22
short 28, 76
shoulder 74
shower 31
shut 32
sight 74
sign-board 10
sign-post 10
silk 54, 56
sink 30
sit down (to) 52
skate (to) 64
skater 79
ski (to) 64
ski-boots 62
ski-cap 62
ski-instructor 62
ski-lift 63
ski-sticks 62
skier 63, 79
skiing 79
skirt 55
skis 62
sky 7
skyscraper 10, 26
sledge 63
sleep (to) 82
sleigh 62
slip (to) 64
slope (ski) 63

89

slow 20
small 28
smell 74
snack-bar 34
snail 67
snake 70
sneeze (to) 64
sniff (to) 72
snow 6, 62
snow (to) 64
snow-cap 62
snowballs 63
snowman 63
sofa 30
sole 43, 74
speak (to) 48
sponge 30
spoon 34
sports 78
square 28
squirrel 66
stairs 31
stand (to) 52
stapler 50
stars 84
station 58
steeple 10
steps 10, 31, 59
stethoscope 75
steward 15
sticking plaster 75
stomach-ache 75
store 11
straight 76
strawberries 42
stream 6
street-lamp 14
strong 76
study (to) 48
subway 14
suit 54
suitcase 14, 18
summer 82
sun 84
sunbathe (to) 83
sunrise 84
sunset 84
supermarket (at the) 38
sweater 55
sweets 42
swim (to) 72, 83
swimming 79
swimming-pool 27, 79
swing (to) 72
switch-board 50
switchboard operator 22, 50
syringe 75

T

T-shirt 55
table 30, 34
table-cloth 34
tablets 75
tails 68
take (to) 44, 82
take a bus (to) 20
take off (to) 56
take photographs (to) 82
talk (to) 48
tall 28, 76
tanker 19
taste 74
taxi-driver 22
teacher 46
teacher's desk 46
teaspoon 34
technician 22
telephone 50
television aerial 10
television set 30
temple 74
tennis 78
terrace 26
theatre 11
there 58
thermometer 75
thigh 74
thin 76
think (to) 48
through 58
throw (to) 80
throw away (to) 12
thumb 74
thumb a lift (to) 20
ticket-collector 14
tidy 28
tie 54
tins 39
toilet 31
toll gate 19
tomatoes 43
tongue 74
tooth 74
toothache 75
toothbrush 31, 75
toothpaste 75
top floor 11
tortoise 66
touch 74
tower 10
town 10, 26
town hall 10
traffic sign 11, 19
trailer truck 19
train 14
travel (to) 16

trees 6
trolley 38
trousers 54
trunk 18, 68
turkey 67
type (to) 52
typewriter 50
typist 22, 50

U

ugly 76
under 58
underground car park 11
untidy 28
up 58

V

van 38
vegetable 39
vegetable stall 43
veranda 27
village 6
vinegar 35
visit (to) 12
vulture 71

W

wait (to) 12
waiter 35
waiting-room 58
waitress 22, 35
wake up (to) 32
walk (to) 12
wall 31, 32
wallet 18, 38
wardrobe 31
wart-hog 70
wash (to) 32
waste-paper 46
water tank 18
water-melon 42
waterfall 6
wave (to) 16
weak 76
weigh (to) 44
whiskers 68
white 8
wicker basket 18
wide 28
wind-sock 15
wind-cheater 54, 62
wind-surfer 79
wind-surfing 79
windows 15, 31, 32
wing 15, 68
with 58
without 58
wood 7, 27

wool 56
woollen 54, 55
work (to) 22, 24
workman 23
worm 67
wrap up (to) 44
wrist 74
write (to) 48
writing-desk 50

Y

yellow 8
young 76

Z

zebra 70
zip 56

SOLUTIONS

Page 7: 1. wrong, 2. wrong, 3. right, 4. wrong, 5. right, 6. right, 7. wrong.

Page 8: Save nature.

Page 9: 1. The sky is light blue, 2. The trees are green, 3. The snow is white, 4. The river is blue, 5. The mountains are purple, 6. The fields are brown, 7. The rocks are grey, 8. The flowers are red.

Page 10 and 11: 1. yes, 2. no, 3. yes, 4. yes, 5. no, 6. yes, 7. yes, 8. yes, 9. no, 10. no.

Page 12: You can park your car in the parking area near the railway station and walk into the centre of the town. There you can visit the Town Hall and photograph the old tower and the church with the steeple. If you cross the road at the pedestrian crossing you arrive at a big store with four floors. In the evening you can meet your friends at the theatre. After the show you can wait at the bus stop for a bus to the railway station where you parked your car.

Page 13: *Game A:* 1. walk, 2. photograph, 3. visit a museum, 4. cross the road, 5. park, 6. post, 7. meet, 8. throw away.
Game B: 1. meet, 2. photograph, 3. cross, 4. visit, 5. walk, 6. throw, 7. park, 8. post.

Page 16: 1. aeroplane, wing, windsock, window, air terminal - 2. hostess, steward, hangar, runway, rudder - 3. subway, platform, railway lines, trolley, compartment - 4. carriage, engine, bridge, train, luggage.

Page 17: I packed my suitcase and took my passport. Then I travelled by bus to the airport. I like to look out of the window of the aeroplane and the hostess is always very kind! I'd like to be a pilot or work in the control tower. Oh no! I've forgotten my ticket.

Page 19: 1. tanker, 2. frontier, 3. bridge, 4. lorry, 5. truck, 6. motorway, 7. suitcase, 8. trunk, 9. handbag, 10. purse, 11. basket, 12. wallet.

Page 20: 1. true, 2. false, 3. true, 4. true, 5. false, 6. false, 7. false, 8. false, 9. false, 10. true.

Page 21: A car.

Page 23: 1. A shop-assistant sells things to people, 2. A petrol-pump attendant fills up your car, 3. A bus-driver drives his bus. 4. A porter carries a bag or a suitcase, 5. A secretary works in an office, 6. A computer operator pushes the keys on her computer.

Page 24: All work and no play makes Jack a dull boy.

Page 25: 1. When an architect draws a plan he uses a set square and a ruler, 2. When a mechanic repairs a car, he sometimes uses a spanner, 3. You can fill up your car at a petrol pump, 4. A housewife buys food and carries it home in a shopping bag, 5. When a policeman directs the traffic he sometimes uses a whistle.

Page 27: 1. false, 2. false, 3. true, 4. true, 5. false, 6. false, 7. true.

Page 28: *Game A:* 1. old, 2. clean, 3. cold, 4. dirty, 5. few, 6. dark, 7. round, 8. narrow, 9. wide, 10. untidy, 11. tall, 12. new, 13. light, 14. hot, 15. short. *Game B:* 1. small, 2. big, 3. tidy, 4. many, 5. square.

Page 29: 1. terrace, 2. building, 3. hospital, 4. chalet, 5. swimming pool, 6. lake, 7. castle, 8. garage, 9. attic, 10. farm, 11. motel, 12. parking area, 13. camper, 14. skyscraper/A car and a caravan.

Page 30 and 31: Hall: back door - carpet - stairs. Kitchen: cooker - refrigerator - sink. Living-room: armchair - fireplace - sofa. Bedroom: bed - rug - wardrobe. Bathroom: bath - shower - toilet. Outside: bell - door mat - steps.

Page 32: You go up the steps to the front door and ring the bell. Your friend opens the door and you go into the hall. In the hall there's a carpet on the floor. On the left there's the living-room. There's a picture on the wall and a television set near the sofa. In one corner there's a table and some chairs and there are some curtains at the window. Your friend goes into the kitchen and makes you a cup of tea while you go into the bathroom to wash your hands. You and your friend walk in the garden before you say "Goodbye".

Page 33: 1. The lamp is under the television set, 2. The cup is near the curtain, 3. The comb is above the window, 4. The hairbrush is between the plant and the television set, 5. The toothbrush is under the sofa.

Page 35: 1. There are three, 2. She's got a tray, 3. He's got his wallet, 4. There are three, 5. There are five, 6. There are five.

Page 36: 1. wrong, 2. right, 3. wrong, 4. wrong, 5. right, 6. right, 7. right, 8. wrong, 9. right, 10. wrong.

Page 37: cash-register, a bread roll, cruet set, waiter, knife, glass, menu, napkin, spoon, fork.

Page 39: 1. There are thirteen people, 2. Seven of them are women, 3. Five of them are men, 4. Only one of them is a child, 5. There are two cashiers, 6. There are eight trolleys, 7. There are two assistants.

Page 40: 1. baker, 2. fishmonger, 3. fruiterer, 4. florist, 5. confectioner, 6. bookseller, 7. butcher, 8. chemist. / A grocer's.

Page 44: 1. c, 2. b, 3. a, 4. c, 5. c, 6. b, 7. a, 8. c.

Page 45: Confectionary.

Page 47: 1. bookshelves, 2. teacher, 3. waste-paper basket, 4. pupil, 5. clothes-peg, 6. school-bag, 7. classroom, 8. calendar.

Page 48: 1. *Down* classroom, 1. *Across* calendar, 2. pupil, 3. pen, 4. blackboard, 5. poster, 6. bag, 7. copy-book, 8. basket, 9. boy, 10. desk,

11. teacher, 12. chair, 13. difficult.
Page 49: A. 7, B. 1, C. 8, D. 2, E. 5, F. 6, G. 3, H. 4.
Page 51: 1. The secretary on the left is operating the switch-board, 2. Another secretary is using a computer, 3. The manager is looking at his notebook, 4. An office-boy is leaving the room, 5. There are a lot of files in this office, 6. The typist and the clerk are talking, 7. There is a photocopier near the door.
Page 52: 1. The manager is introducing the new clerk, Mr Brown. 2. "Telephone at once! Dial four, five, o, nine, seven". 3. The typist comes to the office by bus. 4. "The manager's telephoning at the moment. Please sit down." 5. I've worked all morning and I'm very tired. 6. The switch-board operator always arrives exactly at nine o'clock. She is always on time. 7. Everyone goes home in the evening. 8. "It's ten past nine! You're late." 9. The clerk is standing near the photocopier because he wants to make a copy of a letter. 10. "These letters are urgent. Type them at once, please."
Page 53: A secretary works in an office.
Page 55: 1. With jeans you can wear a shirt, 2. Over a dress you can put on a coat, 3. When it's cold you wear a wind-cheater, 4. With a skirt you can wear a T-shirt, 5. When it's warm you wear a blouse, 6. Men wear a jacket and trousers, 7. On your feet you wear shoes, 8. On your head you can wear a silk scarf.
Page 56: *Game A:* sweater, suit, button-hole, woollen, trousers, dress, cotton.
Game B: 1. silk, 2. skirt, 3. sandals, 4. shoes, 5. suit, 6. shirt, 7. sweater, 8. scarf.
Page 57: A. wind-cheater/boots, B. raincoat/shoes, C. hat/coat, D. jacket/trousers, E. silk scarf/woollen jacket, F. shirt/tie.
Page 59: *Game A:* far - near, on - under, off - on, up - down, with - without, inside - outside, at the front - at the back.
Game B: between, along, through, round.
Page 61: A. 5, B. 7, C. 2, D. 4, E. 9, F. 6, G. 8, H. 3, I. 1.
Page 63: 1. false, 2. false, 3. true, 4. true, 5. false, 6. true.
Page 64: *Game A:* 1. ski, 2. skis, 3. snow, 4. slip, 5. slope, 6. scarf, 7. skier, 8. skate, 9. sticks, 10. sleigh, 11. sledge, 12. shiver, 13. sneeze, 14. snowman, 15. snowballs.
Game B: I'm a snowman!
Page 65: In the picture there is a skier.
Page 67: 1. parrot, 2. pig, 3. turkey, 4. donkey, 5. tortoise, 6. duck, 7. kitten, 8. goat, 9. hen, 10. horse, 11. rabbit, 12. bee, 13. hamster.
Page 68: 1. dog/claws, 2. cock/ears, 3. horse/horns, 4. snail/tail, 5. fish/beak, 6. tortoise/whiskers, 7. hen/hoofs, 8. rabbit/wings, 9. cow/trunk, 10. lamb/mane. The two correctly-drawn animals are the goose and the bird.

Page 71: 1. ostrich, 2. elephant, 3. giraffe, 4. snake, 5. chameleon, 6. zebra, 7. gazelle, 8. dromedary.
Page 72: Animals can't speak, so be kind to them.
Page 73: 1. buffalo, 2. flamingo, 3. giraffe, 4. zebra, 5. dromedary, 6. ostrich, 7. chameleon, 8. crocodile, 9. elephant.
Page 75: 1. true, 2. true, 3. false, 4. false, 5. false, 6. true.
Page 76: *Game A:* long/short, curly/straight, happy/sad, tall/short, old/young, handsome/ugly, thin/fat, dark/fair, strong/weak, left/right.
Game B: 1. calf, 2. palm, 3. pupil, 4. tongue, 5. chest, 6. arms, 7. eye.
Page 77: *Game A:* 1. hair, 2. eyebrow, 3. eye, 4. nose, 5. tooth, 6. chin, 7. neck, 8. shoulder, 9. elbow, 10. hand, 11. thigh, 12. knee, 13. calf, 14. ankle, 15. foot.
Game B: 1. strong, 2. ugly, 3. fat, 4. tall.
Page 79: a) gloves, b) diving-board, c) foil, d) goal, e) apparatus, f) hockey-stick, g) oar, h) net, i) swimming-pool.
Page 80: Practise sports! It's good for your health. It strengthens your muscles and keeps your body fit. You can do exercises every morning, bend and stretch in your bedroom near an open window or throw and catch a ball with your friends in a park or garden. You can play football: kicking the ball makes your knees strong and if you are the goal-keeper and save a lot of goals you strengthen your arms. Other good exercises are lifting weights and shooting but it's best to do these sports with a coach.
Page 81: cycling, skiing, horse-riding, swimming, tennis, football, basket-ball, high-jump, hockey, skating. Pentathlon.
Page 83: 1. picnic, 2. play, 3. cycle, 4. camp, 5. paint, 6. read, 7. swim, 8. walk, 9. climb, 10. collect shells, 11. sleep, 12. fish, 13. sunbathe, 14. do exercises, 15. ride.
Page 84: sea/island, church/steeple, runway/aeroplane, cart/horse, baby/baby-sitter, building/floors, bath/sponge, snackbar/food, check-out/cashier, fruit/vegetables, school/teacher, typist/typewriter, boots/shoes, button/button-hole, snow/sleigh, lamb/sheep, swimming/diving, nose/smell, boxing/gloves, summer/holidays.
Page 85: In summer the sun is warm. It's fun to camp near the sea. You can fish, sunbathe and swim from sunrise to sunset. If it's a cloudy day you can listen to music or read a book. You can sleep under the stars by the light of the moon and in the morning you can wake up to the singing of the birds.

Nature	6
The town	10
An airport railway station	14
Travelling abroad	18
People at work	22
Buildings	26
The house	30
A snack-bar	34
At the supermarket	38
An open-air market	42
In the classroom	46
In the office	50
A fashion-show	54
Here and there	58
A winter scene	62
Pets and farm animals	66
African animals	70
The human body	74
Sports	78
During the summer	82
Wordlist	87
Solutions	91